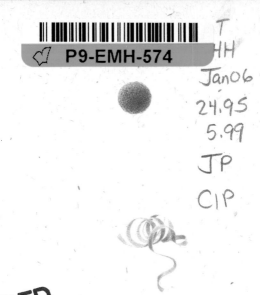

T
HH
Jan06
24.95
5.99
JP
CIP

Illustrations copyright © 2002 by Monique Felix.

Text adapted from poem by Robert Louis Stevenson.

Published in 2002 by Creative Editions, 123 South Broad Street, Mankato,

MN, 56001 USA. Creative Editions is an imprint of The Creative Company.

Designed by Rita Marshall. All rights reserved. No part of the contents

of this book may be reproduced by any means without the written permission

of the publisher. Printed in Italy.

Library of Congress Cataloging-in-Publication Data

Stevenson, Robert Louis., 1850-1894.

My shadow/written by Robert Louis Stevenson; illustrated by Monique Felix.

Summary: An illustrated version of the familiar poem describing the attributes

of a child's shadow. ISBN 1-56846-141-0

1. Shades and shadows—Juvenile poetry. 2. Children's poetry, Scottish.

[1. Shadows—Poetry. 2. Scottish poetry.] I. Felix, Monique, ill. II. Title.

PR5489 .M9 2002   821'.8 dc21   2001047573

9 8 7 6 5 4 3 2

Monique Felix

Robert Louis Stevenson

my Shadow

Creative Editions

I have a little shadow that goes in and out with me,

And what can be the use of him is more than I can see.

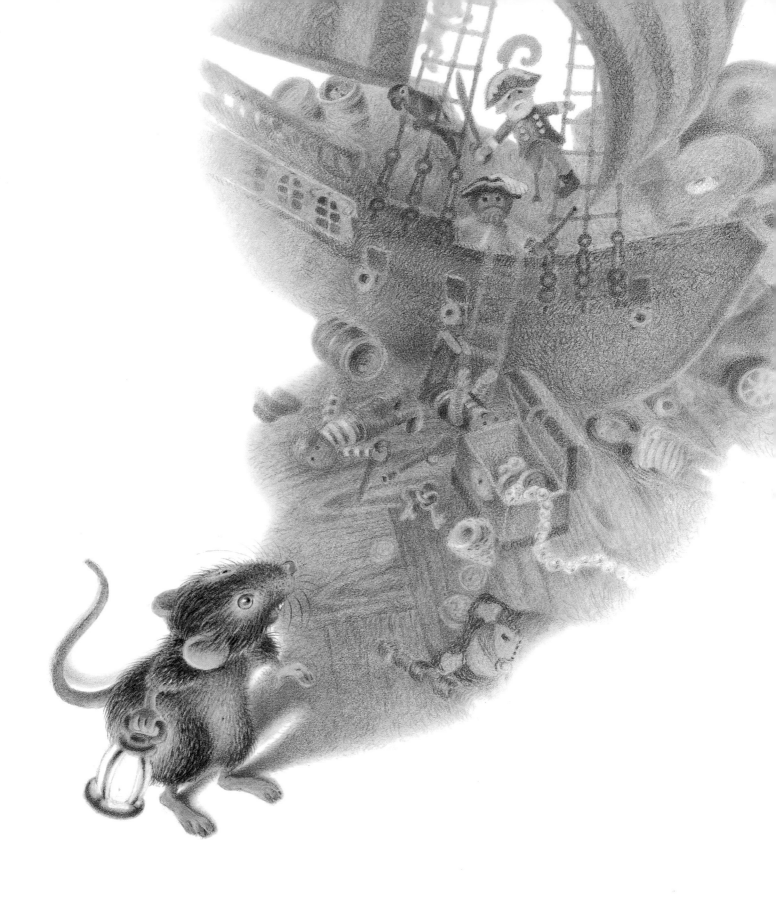

He is very, from the to the

very like me
heels up
head;

And I see him jump before me, when I jump into my bed.

The funniest
him is the way
Not at all like
which is alw

thing about

he likes to grow–

proper mice,

ays very slow;

For he someti

taller like an in

mes shoots up
dia-rubber ball,

And the sometimes gets so little that there's none of him at all.

He hasn't got
a notion of
how mice
ought to
play,

And can only make a fool of me in every sort of way.

He stays so close beside me, the he's a coward you can see;

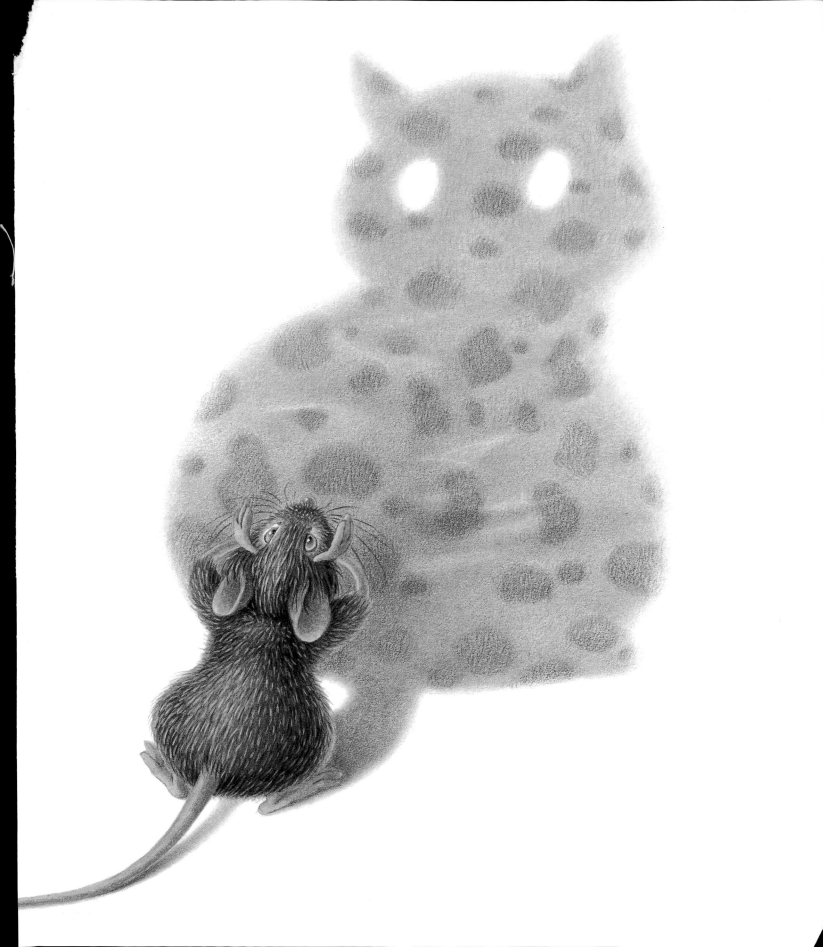

I think I'd shame to stick to mom as that shadow sticks to me!

One morning,
very early,
before the sun
was up,

I rose and found the shining dew on every buttercup;

But my
lazy 🧸 little
shadow, like
an errant
sleepyhead,

Had stayed at home behind me and was fast asleep in bed.

DISCARDED

TOTTENHAM BRANCH LIBRARY